The Poetic Mind Of A Chaotic Soul

For the Ones Who Feel Too Much

Deepshika D

BookLeaf Publishing
India | USA | UK

Made with ❤ on the BookLeaf Publishing Platform
www.bookleafpub.in
www.bookleafpub.com

Dedication

To Mammam (Grandmom), Maa and Sayali: my roots, resilience and wings.

Preface

My name is Sanskrit-derived, and the illuminating prefix of my name—**"Deep"**—means "light" or "lamp" in Sanskrit. Interestingly, "Deep" is also an English word, and it resonates deeply with who I am. I think deeply, sometimes too deeply. I am a keen observer of the world around me, analysing and contemplating. Through both first-hand experiences and moments as a critical observer, I've gained insight into the complexities of life. My strongest suit? I can truly empathise and feel what others feel. And thus, born a poet, starting her very own poetic journey.

This book is a collection of my emotional rollercoasters: of heartbreaks, griefs, scars and unrequited love. The heartbeat behind every line is a search for understanding, a longing to be seen, and a hope that these words might resonate with your own life's music.

Acknowledgements

I would like to thank Bookleaf Publishing for providing this platform to first-time poets.
However, deepest gratitude goes to my patient listeners: my mom and my best friend, Sayali, the real torchbearers during my darkest nights. I would also like to thank my uncle (mama), aunt (mami), brother (bhai) and my friends: Kaushik, Dhananjay, Adit, Prashant, Amirtheswari, Insuvai and Aamrapali.
That being said, I owe this book to every significant being who came into my life; they perhaps stayed or left, but they made me who I am today.

1. Of Silence, Fire and Freedom

The moon shone full and bright,
As the clock struck twelve, I stirred to life.
Bones cracked, fangs gleamed, eyes turned red,
Blood gushed through my veins as I screamed in pain
Distant howls pierced through my ears,
The rage in me sparked a fire.

I can feel the power, I can feel the freedom,
I let out a shrill roar deafening the eardrum.
I broke the shackles that chained me to the ground,
I am no more the gentle girl, the way you found.

As I raced out in the dark, in the bare and wild,
He caught my arms, with a grip so mild,
"Wait", he said, as he held me tight,
"Won't let you go; you are mine tonight."

But there awaits a world, that I now call my home,
Where the souls are free and the wild hearts roam,
They too were humans once, weak and thin,
But the frenzied chaos unleashed the beast within.

I let go of his hands, I never looked back,

I love the bare and wild.
Not a tear was shed, no pain was felt,
The heart didn't want to crawl back this time.

I am the woman you fear,
I don't bow down, my dear,
I have sailed through many ups and downs,
*I **can feel the power, I can feel it within,***
Now that I am a Werewolf, catch me if you can.

2. Of Smiles, Sins and Illusions

'Tis the town of the Dead
Where zombies run free,
Where you breathe in oxygen
But devoid of empathy.

Behind the gracious smile,
You have a heart full of sin,
And beneath that glow of baby pink,
You shelter evil thoughts, as dark as ink.

'Tis the town of the Dead,
Where shallowness reigns at its peak,
Where you hopelessly fall in love,
Only to sway in the very next beat.

This town is vibrant with hues of red and blue,
But the emotions that you show are never true,
Here you may have countless friends
But betrayal will await you in the very end.

'Tis the town of the Dead,
Woven from the threads of illusion,

Don't you hunt here for ghosts at night,
'Cause everyone hides one within.

3. Of Tears, Trials and Triumph

A scarred past, a troubled soul;
Her smile veils her deep wounds,
Screamed in pain, cried in silence,
A weak child from a broken home.

Moments of grief haunted yesterdays,
The people she loved, forever left.
The regrets she bears, the memories she holds,
A living child in a grave so cold.

She dared to dream, she chose to fight,
Amidst the self doubt, against the ruthless time,
The world was cruel, laughed at her fall,
A trembling child, steadfast to her goals.

She broke the chains, stood the test of time,
She rose like a phoenix, fire burning in her eyes.
Seems a gentle girl, delicate and soft,
But in her past, she has calmed several storms.

4. Of Ink, Steel and Revolution

One day, a pen asked the sword,
"Do you kill people when they don't follow your words?"

"I slit their throats and cut them in half,
The defiant is weak, his plight is my laugh
My blade shines with every glorious victory.
In one swish I create history."

The pen led out a derisive grin,
" Oh mighty sword, such pride you take in your radiant sheen,
The intoxicating power has made you blind
I, however, unveil the words untold, hidden in the layers of the mind.
With every move, I create a wave of thought
Which kindled the fire behind every war fought.
Bow down before me, for I am the beacon of evolution,
You may silence the voice, but I spark a revolution"

5. Of Scars, Solitude and Serenity

She walked away from something, too broken to bloom,
A mirror amidst a desert, reflecting the deepest wounds.
A weird feeling of love, yet felt like a storm,
A sense of calmness, as the ties were torn.
A disturbed mind knew its own kind,
A soul felt familiar, the heart ached, yet cared.
The deep emotions kept cutting through her veins,
Yet every silence felt softer than the noise of their presence.
A daring step to end, the answer she knew,
The ask was the exit, finally, she can bloom.
They would see her clearly even in the darkest nights,
In the end, she escaped from herself, with no desire to be found.

6. Of Griefs, Haunts and Hope

Somewhere in the darkest corner of my heart,
Where the light never creeps in, a Hades' underworld.
Lies the faded memories, deeply treasured,
Hidden in the webs of unkept promises and desires.

In the darkest moments, when nostalgia descends,
I dig my heart to reach that place.
A union with the people who once left,
A travel to the past where nothing seems changed.
Ephemeral are the journeys of these fleeting lives.
Yet the memories remain not burnt, just buried alive.

7. Of Chaos, Chant and Calm

Crushed by the burden of unspoken thoughts,
Seeking peace in the corners of this dark world.
A fiery storm raging within,
My mind is in chaos, deep wounds bleeding.
Caught in the threads of worldly attachments,
Seeking isolation amidst this cluttered existence.

As the facade of illusions crumbles to pieces,
The chant of "Om" echoes through the night's stillness,
The despair fades, paving the way to calm.
God, before you, I humbly surrender.

8. Of Beliefs, Science and War

The temples of worship,
where we wash our sins,
The faiths we follow,
Do they not all preach peace?
The science of the classrooms,
Which gave birth to curious minds,
The philosophers of history,
Did they not urge us to seek, "What, How and Why?"

We all grew up together, In this continuum of time;
Reading the same Books of the religion
And the same Laws of science.

Then what went wrong,
That led to this mental haze,
Why has this present World,
Turned into a ball of sprawling mess?
Why are all sane people turning insane?
Why are rational minds choosing irrationality over reason?
Why are we losing ourselves in search of bliss?
And why does our blood boil, when our religions choose peace?

As I sit in the dark,
With a million questions in my head,
If we were taught the same things,
Why some of us learnt so different?

9. Of Seas, Strangers and Family

As I took one step out of the door,
A sudden epiphany, I am never coming back home.
I embraced the new waves, and bid adieu to the shore,
As the ship stirred awake, I embarked on the voyage alone.

The miles once feared, paved the way to a town,
Full of strangers, soon they would be known.
The moments, though fleeting, were woven into memories,
As life unfurled its chapters, we wrote new stories.
First hellos and timid smiles turned to deeper bonds.
Thus born a new family, and the house evolved into a home.

As specks of sand descend the glass,
The mound beneath speaks of the time that has passed,
I remembered the house across the seven seas,
The house that harbours my childhood, where I once dared to dream.
The fragile walls echo the laughters we shared,
The weathered objects hold the touch of those no longer there.

As I yearn for that house, which was once my home,
Will those four walls still feel the same, when I return to roam?

10. Beyond the Binary

He was a bit different,
"Odd", as people would say,
While boys raced their cars,
He braided the doll's hair, all day.

"I am like my mom", often he said,
With pride, he embraced femininity, is that a mistake he made?
Disowned and abandoned, he was thrown in the streets.
Harassed and shamed, he is a woman, and that's how you treat?

He begs for a living, he dares not to dream
He lives in a dark slum and shares his only meal.
Weird, it is right, the way he claps?
Don't you burst in laughs when he wears a saree and dance?
But there beats a human heart behind his coarse voice.
How different would his life be if given a choice?

11. Of Despair, Betrayal and Hope

The day we met,
Hard I fell,
Deep into the ocean of reckless insanity,
Fingers crossed, hopes soared up,
When will our paths collide again.

Dark past lurking,
Tainted memories smirking,
The voice in my head pierced the calmness
With a devious grin,
Utter madness she screamed,
Don't you dare to fall into that trap,

For once, you loved a boy and gave your all,
But did it end the way you thought?
One night, when the thunder struck and the storm raged,
And the ominous clouds cursed your name,
Behind the tall trees, he appeared with a relentless speed,
With a shimmering sword, he stabbed your heart,
You cried in pain, you bled till death,
You let go of dreams you once dreamt,
You stared at the vast empty of nothingness
And questioned your very existence

And now that you see a glistening hope,
How can you be so certain-
That he is the one to free your spirits
From your tormented past?
Or merely an embodiment of the devil
Waiting to betray you again,
Leaving you with a broken heart and soul-scarring pain.

Will this winter ever blossom into a new spring?

12. Of Eternal Nights and Transient Bonds

Under the sea of shimmering stars,
Holding hands, two restless hearts.
Gazing at the Milky Way; counting the dots,
A celestial witness to this forbidden love?
Cigarettes in hand, conversations so deep,
A moment caught in this eternal drift.
The Magpies bowed before Chronos might,
A union of two souls for one last night.
A silent whisper: this should never fade.
As the eyes met, a connection was felt.

13. Of Blood and Frost

A wounded soul detached from the truest desires,
A hollow heart, stuck in the past, once full of love,
A lustful mind, craving bodies, just afraid to be loved.
A ruthless man, hiding a timid boy beneath layers of pride.
Often misunderstood, he wears a veil to cover his unseen scars.
Terrified to be seen, bruised by his own reflection,
Once, a heartless girl fell for a vessel, already cracked and bleeding.

14. Of Hurt, Healing and Growth

Never loved, always the one to give,
Sits in the darkness, never forgets yet forgives.
A chaotic poet, writing verses for the beloved,
Often misunderstood, offering empathy to the undeserved,
Fell for a heart, too empty to love,
Cares for those not worthy of her warmth.
Sees through the disturbed souls, only to bleed in return,
Gets herself drowned, to save the people already sunk.
But after the storm, often comes the calm,
She walks away from those who failed to be human,
Reluctant to bend to make others whole,
Once a healer, now ready to be healed.

15. Mind over Body

There she goes - striding on the streets,
In a red crop top and bell-bottom jeans,
"Oh my god- look at her rack!"
Whispered a man, on the crowded tracks.
Greedy eyes and a lustful mind,
The men gazed at her: old and young alike.

As she stopped to buy a meal,
A dude groped her ass, tried to cope a feel.
Two old ladies smirked from behind,
"Those tight jeans: sluts deserve that kind"
She shows her cleavage, you think, she has a brain?
She does too much makeup,
Probably she just sleeps with men.

She can be a scholar or changing the world,
But why show her respect, when looks are what you care!
If her beauty fits the standards, don't hesitate to stare.
Else, feel free to criticise, mocking her with a glare.

This is an urge to all dear men,
Look beyond than what your two teeny eyes can,
She does cherish the body she proudly owns,

But let's not forget the brilliance that she has grown.

And to the ladies who shamefully judge;

If you can change your thought

With grace, I welcome you to this modern world.

16. Of Grace and Honor

To every girl with a romantic heart,
Who falls so deep, just to get hurt,
Take a moment, and know your worth,
Let the silence speak and not your words.
For love is bold, and love is free,
Let him go if he is weak.
A strong man won't leave you alone,
If he is worthy, he will show.
If you beg and if you plead,
He will hesitate in times of need
When storms will rise, he will not fight,
The fleeting tides will make him scare.
So stand in grace and stand tall,
You are one in a billion, not meant to fall.
If he's worthy, he will see;
Just for you, he will cross the seven seas.

17. Of Solitude and Detachment

As I sit on the bench, lost in the wind's whispered hymn,
A moment of solitude, why it feels so serene?
A thousand thoughts dissolve into stillness,
Amidst the chaos, seeking a language of silence.
Observing the world, just as it is,
One deep breath, as the time keeps rushing.
Vibing with the cacophony, lost in the words unsaid,
As the world makes noise, I remain disconnected.

18. Of Forgotten Spring and Abandoned Love

Lost in the sea of countless men,
I am a tiny speck in the desert's hand
If you ever find me crossing your path
Pretend I am a stranger, and don't look back.
I was a memory, now burnt to ashes.
A spike in your lifeline, as time flashes.
Withered petals of a flower, now buried deep in the earth.
A path that was taken, but abandoned at last.
Cheers to the good time, and a final goodbye.
I am a forgotten spring, in seasons of your life.

19. Of Daunting Journeys and Eternal Paradise

As I stand on the precipice,
A fear of the unknown consumes me from within,
One wrong step, and I sink into a dark abyss,
Yet inaction unfolds into a myriad of opportunities amiss.
The flame of self-belief lights up the path unexplored,
Guiding the inner self towards a daunting ascent,
For in the end lies the world of eternal paradise,
The courage within pulls me out of the dubious haze.

20. Of Freedom and Space

Breathe in, breathe out,
Someone calm my head,
I yearn for freedom, I crave for space.

Don't you love the independence, when you are alone?
Free from the shackles of ties, with no one to rely on.
I am in my twenties, I have goals ahead,
I want to travel the world before I am bound or wed.

To all the boys I have dated:
I did my best,
I valued the friendship,
But I despised the rest.

The idea of "we" suffocates me,
Why do I need a boyfriend, when I can just be me?
Phone calls, conflicts, misunderstandings and strife
Oh my god, it takes up so much of your life!!
Rather, I would pursue those ten hobbies of mine,
Man! I love it when I have so much of free time!

I do like romance: do not get me wrong,
I cry at happy endings and listen to emo songs,
But being with someone burdens me,

I feel I am chained, someone please set me free!

So what do I do if I meet a new guy?

Pretend to be heartless, and go on in my life!

www.ingramcontent.com/pod-product-compliance
Lightning Source LLC
Chambersburg PA
CBHW051752130826
49812CB00033B/1123
9789370924000